YOUNG PEOPLE OF THE BIBLE

The River Baby

Text by BETTY SMITH
Art by NORM HAMDORF

LUTTERWORTH PRESS
GUILDFORD AND LONDON

First British Edition 1980
Copyright © 1978 Lutheran Publishing House, Adelaide.
Printed in Hong Kong

"Listen, Miriam —
is that baby crying?"

"I think so."

"Quickly, run and pick
him up. If anyone hears him,
we'll all be killed."

Long ago, the great River
Nile flowed through the land
of Egypt just as it does today.
Coming from high mountains,
it swept swiftly through the
rapids. Then it widened out and
ran more slowly as it passed
great cities on its way to the sea.

The king of that country (who was
called the Pharaoh) had thousands of
slaves. They came from another
country and were called Hebrews. They
were treated very cruelly. They had to
work terribly hard, making bricks,

pulling big statues into position and building huge temples. Beside them stood the foremen, called task-masters. They carried whips to use on slaves if they didn't work hard enough.

Each night, the Hebrews prayed to God and asked Him to help them. Every morning they wondered what would happen during the day. Fathers and mothers, boys and girls were taken away from each other. They were always miserable and sad. Then, instead of getting better, things became worse. The slaves found the Pharaoh was even more cruel than they had thought possible.

He had so many slaves he thought they might rebel and fight against him. He didn't want *that* to happen. He made a plan to stop the Hebrew boys from growing up. The wicked order was given — to throw every baby boy into the river as soon as he was born. Oh, how sad the poor slaves were! Now they prayed more and more often to God, asking that He should send someone to help them escape.

One day, a new baby boy was born in one of the little Hebrew huts. Mother and father loved him so much, they couldn't bear to carry out the king's order. So, for three months, they hid him in their house. Their two older children, Miriam and Aaron, helped to look after the baby. Every time he cried they rushed to pick him up. They pressed his little face against them to deaden the noise. Always they thought, "Suppose an egyptian is passing!" "Suppose someone hears baby!" They knew if that happened they would all die.

By the time baby was three months old, it wasn't possible to quieten him so easily. He was growing bigger every day. The family knew they couldn't hide him any longer. They all asked God to show them a way to save their baby. And God put an idea into their minds.

Mother took the reeds (or bulrushes) which grew along the river bank. She made them into a basket with a lid. Then she spread bitumen all over the basket to make it waterproof. It was like a lovely little boat.

One morning, very early, before anyone else was awake, Mother and sister Miriam set off. Mother carried baby and Miriam the basket. When they reached the river, they waded in and Miriam laid the basket on the water. It floated so well that not one drop of water leaked into it. Then Mother put some soft old cloths in the bottom and gently laid her little baby on them.

There he lay, just as cosy and comfy as if he were in a cot. Mother bent over him for a long moment. She prayed to God to keep her little one safe.

"O Lord God of my people," she whispered. "Please keep my baby safe from all harm and danger.
Take him into Your care.
Bless him so that he
may grow up to love
and serve You."

Then she
closed the
lid and said
to Miriam,
    "Now, watch to see
what happens. Stay out
of sight among the reeds.
You can follow the basket
as the river carries it along."
    That is just what Miriam
did. The little basket bobbed
up and down in the water
and the rocking sent baby
to sleep. When it moved, Miriam

moved too,
wading through
the shallow water
near the bank.
When it was
halted by the
reeds or a little
patch of calm
water, she
stood still.

Presently she heard the
sound of voices, laughing
and talking. She pushed
aside the reeds and peered
out. Down a flight of
steps cut into the bank
of the river, came
a group of girls.

When Miriam saw the girl in the centre, her heart beat faster. The others had pretty dresses, but *hers* was beautiful! They wore ornaments, but precious jewels sparkled in her head-dress — in the lovely collar she wore — in the rings on her fingers. No wonder Miriam was afraid. This was the Pharaoh's daughter. She was the <u>Princess</u> of Egypt.

As the girls began to prepare for their bath, a ripple caught the basket. It carried it out from among the reeds. The Princess saw it.

"What's that?" she asked, pointing.

All her ladies-in-waiting looked too. What could it be, they wondered. Finally, the Princess asked one of them to wade in and bring the basket to her. Without opening it, the girl pulled it back to the bank.

The Egyptian girls lifted the basket on to the edge of the steps. The Princess herself lifted the lid. What a surprise she had! She looked at the baby lying there and suddenly he woke up. The rocking had stopped. There he lay with strange faces all around him. It was too much for the poor baby. Tears filled his big, brown eyes and he began to cry.

Miriam was really frightened. Suppose the Princess was like her father! Suppose she threw baby back into the river!

But the Princess was *not* like her father. She was good and kind and wouldn't hurt the little one. She looked at the others.

"This is one of the Hebrew children," she said quietly. "Someone has done this to save him from the king's order."

With a quick
movement, she picked
baby up and cuddled
him. His sobs died away
and he clung closely to
her. The Princess smiled
as she stroked his little
head. She was lonely. She
had no one to love. And
she decided, then and
there, to keep the baby
sent to her so strangely.
He would be known
as her son, and,
because of that,
he would be
Prince of Egypt.

"I'll call him Moses," she told the girls as they gathered round her, "because I drew him out of the water."

(For the name "Moses" means just that — "drawn out".)

But the Princess knew that she couldn't be with the baby always. She

had many official duties to perform. She needed a nurse who would look after him.

"I wonder where I could find someone who would be my son's nurse?" she asked.

Miriam heard her. Pushing aside the reeds, she ran out. She knelt at the Princess' feet.

"Your Highness." she said breathlessly. "I know a Hebrew woman who'd come if you wanted her."

The Princess must have wondered why a little girl had been hiding in the bulrushes.

She must have known Miriam had listened and she guessed the reason. But she was very kind and wise. So she just smiled and said, "Thank you, my child. Please ask her to come at once."

Miriam ran off quickly. Presently back she came to where the Princess waited. With her was — yes, her own mother.

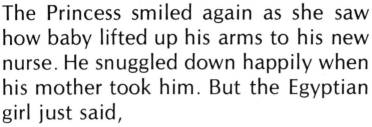

The Princess smiled again as she saw how baby lifted up his arms to his new nurse. He snuggled down happily when his mother took him. But the Egyptian girl just said,

"Would you be willing to look after this baby for me? Of course, you'll be paid for being his nurse."

Would she be willing! The mother's eyes filled with tears as she held her little son. Now she would be able to watch him grow up. Now she knew no one would harm him.

God had saved Moses
to carry out a very special
work. Although he grew up
as a Prince, he found his
own Hebrew people again
when he became a man.
He was the answer to their
prayers for help. Moses learnt
to love and serve God and
became one of the greatest
men who ever lived. In time
God showed him how to
lead his people back to
their own country. There they
could be free and happy
once again.